Now he knew why he loved her so.
Without ever leaving the ground,
she could fly.

— Toni Morrison, <u>Song of Solomon</u>

Elvis Alves

This Is What I Know

Copyright © 2023 by Elvis Alves
All rights reserved by Mahaicony Books.

To reproduce selections from this book, contact:

    Elvis.O.Alves@gmail.com
    www.elvisalves.com

Book design by Tishon Woolcock
Set in TT2020 Style E

Photograph by JB Dodane © jbdodane.com
has been cropped to create the cover art.

Alves, Elvis
This Is What I Know / Elvis Alves
ISBN 978-0-9884324-3-7

For family and friends,
near and far.

Oshosi is the protector. He clears pathways.
The colors blue and yellow are associated
with him.

Blue

We shower the room with blue light
as the child sleeps in her crib.

In this world, you need protection
from everything.

For life to begin, we swim a channel
of waves clashing into each other until
fertilization.

Hand me what belongs to me or step
aside and let me get it.

Stand and watch everything reveal itself
and act accordingly.

Shango is quick tempered. He is associated with lightning, thunder, fire, dance, and virility. His colors are red and white.

Red

There is life in blood. My mother
sprinkles us with the blood of Jesus in
her prayers.

Red is the color of anger. Red is the color
of power. Red is the color of love. And
love is everything.

I have seen doctors pump blood into bodies—
resurrection in plain sight.

Hope flies on the wings of a red bird. Its mouth
belts sweet songs of joy and sorrow like a
sparrow.

Obatala is the owner of the head and mind.
He is associated with creativity and purity.
His main color is white.

White

Color of the afterlife.
Of the world of spirits
and ancestors.

Gather close and hear.
Gather close and learn.

The women dressed in
white worship at the sea.
They pray for help and
protection.

Clairvoyance—to carry the
present into the future with
wind of change.

There is a spiritual reason
behind everything.

Wade in the water.

Life is fine.
The dawn and night
are the same.

Same rising. Like the
burning fire whose flames
rise with the beating of
the drums and the dancing
feet of the women in a circle.

The colors red and purple are also associated with Obatala.

Oshun embodies fertility. She is associated with water. She is the little sister of Yemaya. Her colors are yellow and gold.

Yellow

Not just the sun.
Walk with fierceness that is
a force. People will be jealous
of your confidence because it
belongs to you.

There are dimensions only
you can enter. Keep moving.
The gods know where you are
going even if you do not know.

The ancestors are your guides.
They have worn your clothes.
Have carried you over land and
beneath water before you were
born.

Orunmila is associated with wisdom and divination. His colors are green and yellow.

Green

Verdant. Who sees a field of
green and not want to leave?
The leave-taking is never enough.
Life has a way of surprising us.

I bend my knees to the ground.
Dust swallows my thoughts.
I refuse to stay put. The day
pushes me forward. I walk into
the light and become light.

My head pivots this and that way.
The waves toss. The homes burn.
Renewal is through fire and birth
(rebirth).

Spring brings flowers, green grass,
new thoughts, and an archipelago
of emotions. I pick up the parts
and build a whole. And leave it
behind.

Elegba guards doors and pathways. His colors are black, white, and red.

Black

I return and open The Door of
No Return. The tour guide gives
me a high-five.

This is where they left and never returned.

People pushed into the New World with
blood and sweat and tears.

Free labor built the New World. Free labor
was birthed by capitalism. Capitalism birthed
free labor.

What to the negro is the New World if he
is not free?

They were shipped to plantations. Worked as
slaves until the grave.

There is no pie in the sky. I want to eat my
full in the here and now and not in the bye
and bye.

Black skin grows maps that point to Africa—
land not forgotten. A land alive in the blood.

Sweet home Guinea. Sweet home Ghana.
Black Africans in the New World referred to
Africa as Guinea—a land they came from
and wanted to return to.

I return and open The Door of No
Return. The tour guide gives me a high-five.

This is where enslaved Africans were pushed
into the New World.

A man dressed in white sits in the middle of
the dungeon. He keeps watch.

Never again says the tour guide.

I think of what is birthed in the dark
beyond the light. And open the door.

Red

We wear Shango's robe.
Memories live in blood,
head and heart.

What makes you bleed?
What are you remembering
beyond forgetting and forgiving?

Stay there. Make emblems with
embers that spark fire.

Praise for Yemaya

Mother to earth and all
that gives birth, teach us
in your infinite wisdom
how to be fierce—and
fight for what is right.

Your beauty radiates
with the sun and can't
be undone.

Embrace your children
with compassion and
let them grow from it.

And use their strength—
that comes from you—
to stand for justice, in
defending the weak and
bringing about equality.

Then we will know peace.
And will sing your praise,
raise your name to the
heavens.

This Is What I Know was influenced by a trip to Ghana in 2016 and the symbolism of colors in the Yoruba spiritual tradition. I am interested in how modes of spirituality and literature give context to colors in figurative and literal ways.

Other works by Elvis Alves:

Bitter Melon (2013)

Ota Benga and Other Poems (2017)

I am no Battlefield but a Forest of Trees Growing (2018)

Black/White: We are not Panic (Pandemic) Free (2020)

Blackfish (2022)

Made in United States
North Haven, CT
20 August 2024

56304137R00018